PRAISE FOR
ALDEN R. CARTER'S
DOGWOLF:

"The smoke, dryness, and heat of a summer of western forest fires provide the backdrop for this intense novel about a young man's search for his past and his future.... this is an excellent book...."
— *Booklist*, boxed review

"Carter is a master of tempo and dynamic — the book's pacing is exquisite, giving the readers a chance to absorb the landscape and culture of his characters...."
— *Marshfield News-Herald*

"...a beautifully written story about a 15-year-old, part Indian, part white, in the woods of northern Wisconsin.... The book is on its way to joining the hosts of young-adult classics."
— *Houston Chronicle*

"Strong on images and emotion, this is a haunting book...."
— *School Library Journal*

"Realistic dialogue contains the damns of young men and demonstrates a supportive, amiable family relationship between Pete, his mother, and stepfather."
— *VOYA*

D0204134

Other POINT SIGNATURE
paperbacks you will enjoy:

Dakota Dream
by James Bennett

Arilla Sun Down
by Virginia Hamilton

Freak the Mighty
by Rodman Philbrick

Toning the Sweep
by Angela Johnson